4.4.7

Also edited by Ray Siegener

The Basketball Skill Book

The Basketball

EDITED BY RAY SIEGENER

EARL MONROE
& WES UNSELD

Skill Book

NEW YORK   1974   ATHENEUM

Photographs, unless otherwise indicated, are by Len Kamsler

94273

Contents

The authors wish to give special acknowledgment to Ted Monica, Athletic Director of Madison High School, Madison, New Jersey, for his invaluable assistance in the preparation of this book. Acknowledgment is also made to the staff of Newark Academy, Livingston, New Jersey, for the generous use of their facilities for photography purposes.

The Basketball Skill Book

Introduction

A N Y B O Y W H O has played basketball knows
that it is a game of cooperation. It is a group of
guys getting together and working toward a single
goal. This is the team concept. Being on a team
means, to some degree, that you forget the word
"individual." When the team wins, when the team
is successful, individual recognition comes. As professional basketball players, we must view winning
as all-important because winning is what we are
paid to do. But for young players like you, there
are other factors.

There is consolation in a good job—in doing
your best. If you lose a ball game, if you and your
team have done your best, if you've lost to the right
opponent, you will feel that you have won something even though you may have lost the game. It
depends on your goals.

Your goals right now should be to have fun and

develop your basketball skills. That's the purpose of this book . . . to teach you the skills that will make you a successful team player. Passing, dribbling, shooting, rebounding, defense: these are the ingredients that make a basketball player. The more you can develop in each of these areas, the more nearly you can approach what every coach dreams of: the complete player. Guys like the Lakers' Jerry West, the Bucks' Kareem Jabbar, and the Knicks' Walt Frazier. They can do it all.

All successful athletes work hard at their sport. In basketball, this means spending hours practicing dribbling and passing, perfecting your shots and learning new ones, and improving your defensive skills. Ask any outstanding ballplayer and he'll tell you he's done this. But he will also tell you that he never really thought of it as work. He was doing the thing he loved most. This is probably the other prime ingredient in a great ballplayer—he loves the game.

We all know that we enjoy doing what we do well, so get with it and learn the basics of basketball and learn them correctly. Then, when you find that you are one of the players everyone wants on his team, you will be motivated to work even harder to improve your skills. But first and foremost, get out on the court and have fun.

1. Earl Monroe– The Backcourt Man

I DIDN'T GET started in basketball until I was fourteen and, of course, a lot of the other kids had been playing for five or six years. Because I got a late start in the game, I had a lot of catching up to do. I remember the guys used to laugh at me when I came on the court and I used to be an alternate pick on the playgrounds, which was rather bad for my ego.

My first big decision was to choose between soccer and basketball. I decided that my chances for success were better in basketball, but soccer was one of the things that helped my game. I played soccer for four or five years, up until my senior year in high school. Soccer developed my wind, enabling me to go at a faster pace than a lot of other guys. In the early fall I played soccer and it built up my endurance. By the end of the soccer season I was into basketball and I was already pretty much in shape.

I played center in high school and it wasn't until later, between high school and college, that I found I could play a backcourt position. The experience at the center was very valuable for my game. I was a six-foot-one center at that time and many of the guys I was playing against were bigger. The only way I could shoot around or over them was to have all kinds of funny little moves. This was a big help in the development of my game.

I think the most beneficial year of my career was the year I changed from center to guard. (Ironically, when I was younger, I was considered a stand-out defensive player. Now I'm considered basically an offensive player.) When I moved to guard, I had to reevaluate my basketball skills. I had to learn to dribble the ball and to drive. I also had to learn to shoot from the outside, and, most important, I had to learn to think as a guard.

I'd practice dribbling around the court right-handed at full speed a couple of times, then I'd turn and dribble around the court left-handed at full speed. Another drill I practiced was to do a figure eight within the court, going around the two

6

foul circles and around the circle in the middle of the court.

One thing that helped my dribbling was that most of the playgrounds we played on had a lot of cracks in the cement and the ball would often bounce at crazy angles, so I had to develop fast hands and quick reflexes. When the ball hit the cracks, I had to learn to go with it and get it back under control. This was very beneficial for my type of game, for getting in and out of tight spots.

Shooting was another thing I practiced. I had to learn how to shoot the ball from the outside. When I was a center, I learned how to do a lot of things with my back to the basket. I developed a lot of shots called "flukey-do" shots. These are basically moves you make to try to get up and under and around your opponent. I practiced them every day for up to ten hours, until, by the time I'd go home, my arm and shoulders were so sore my mother had to rub me down with alcohol. That would help until the next day when I went back out and shot some more. I played practically all night—it was a way to keep my mind occupied.

My main assignment as a guard is to keep the team running . . . to try and make sure everyone gets in the play a little bit. When everyone's in the play the team plays together better. Part of my job

7

is to make sure everyone touches the ball during the game. Each backcourt man has his own style. Lenny Wilkins of Cleveland has the ball most of the time and he directs traffic, which makes him very effective because the guy with the ball is definitely going to be the man to watch. The Knicks' Dick Barnett, on the other hand, doesn't handle the ball that much. He plays a different role. He takes some of the pressure off the other guard because he can hit the outside shot. These are two very crafty backcourt men, but they play two different roles.

When my team gets the ball in a defensive rebound situation, I try to set up as a receiver. After I receive the ball, I try to get the ball up the court as quickly as possible, before the defense has a chance to set. If I'm unable to get the ball up the entire court, it's my job to set up the plays and make sure everyone gets in the play.

A guard also has defensive responsibilities. Often his techniques depend on the type of center his team has. If my team has a center who blocks up the middle, I might influence my man to try to run into the middle. If I know I have a center who doesn't block up the middle too well, I try to keep my man away from the middle . . . to the outside. I try to force him to his weak hand, to his left if

8

he shoots best right-handed or to his right if he shoots best left-handed.

The main thing for you to do right now is to learn the skills outlined in the following chapters. Then you will be a valuable part of your team's offense and defense.

2. Wes Unseld – The Big Man

THE WORST assumption we can make is that the primary responsibility of a big man on offense is shooting. In some instances—if you are a Kareem Jabbar or a Wilt Chamberlain—scoring is pretty easy for you. Those players are major elements in the scoring or shooting part of their teams' offense. But more important, as an offensive threat, is what you do without the ball—sometimes without even touching the ball.

A big man's job from the center position (and this also applies to the big forward) is basically to take his place in an offensive pattern. He is not actually running the pattern the way a guard like Earl Monroe would. His job is to see that the pattern is carried out and to deliver the "roadblocks," that is, to see that any defensive man is stopped so that his offensive man can get the shot off. He does this by picks, legally blocking the defensive player, or by shadowing, putting himself in a position not so much where he is setting a pick but rather where the offensive man can run the defensive man off him. He is in the way as a roadblock.

The offense of the big man will not always involve him with the ball. The primary thing for the offense is to have the ball and this is where the big man is very important, especially from the center position. The center or big forward has to get the ball and put it where his teammates can use it. Once the opponents' shot is taken, he goes up to get the rebound. Then he initiates the offense by throwing an outlet pass or getting the ball in a position where a teammate can get it down to the offensive end to score.

The shot that is most important for the big man, although many are getting away from it, is the hook shot. I think the hook shot is the only unblockable shot in the game. This is a great shot for the big man because it delivers him into the basket as close as possible. It provides an adequate defense for the ball by using the shooter's body, and it allows him a very soft and short shot that is most effective.

Another shot that a big man should learn to execute is really not a shot. I am referring to the tip-in. He should learn to control the ball with his fingertips around the basket and in positions that are sometimes unstable or uncomfortable. He should practice jumping and tipping at the same time, then jumping and tipping when off-balance. The idea is to keep the ball alive, to keep the ball up on the backboard, which is a tremendous offensive tactic.

Other shots that the big man will use around the basket are turn-around jump shots from the top of the key, turn-around jump shots while crossing the line, and small fade-away shots to allow a smaller man to shoot over a taller defender. Of course, he should know and practice all the basic shots. But he should concern himself primarily with play in and around the basket. This is where the big man in basketball is supposed to be.

The center, by definition, is the center of all the activity. He is always in the offense whether he is shooting or not. He is the sole stable force around which everybody moves on the court and he has to put himself in a position where he is not in the way but is part of the action. He must always impress on his teammates and himself that, whether or not he's involved in the play, he is the center of the attack. If not, he's going to be the cluck who is out in the middle of the floor clogging up the play.

The center probably has the most important defensive job in basketball. The action flows around and is channeled into the center position. For this reason there's little room once you get into the key area and you need a person who can clog up that middle and keep any unmolested shots from going toward the basket. The center's job on defense is to guard his man but also to help out his guards and forwards. It is up to him to deflect a shot or to put a person off-balance so he cannot get a good shot off.

The center's major responsibility on defense is rebounding. Since he is the closest person to the basket most of the time, he has to get up and get the ball once the shot is taken. From the center position, he is the man who can see all the action at one glance. The center can see both forwards and both guards. It is up to him to call instructions to his defensive men as he observes situations developing.

The responsibilities of a forward are not unlike those of the center and not unlike those of a guard. They are the in-between men: what we'll call a cross between a guard and a center. They have the responsibility of scoring and setting up plays. For instance, the guard's duty is to bring the ball down and try to set up the action. The center's job, if he's not the shooting center, is to initiate picks, initiate the action, and keep it going. But a forward's job is somewhere in between. He has to be able to set up the action and often enough be in on the shooting aspect of the action. He has to be versatile; he has to be able to think fast and react quickly to varied situations on the court because he is this in-between type of ballplayer.

The object of defense from the forward position is to keep the offensive team out of a scoring area. Forwards do this by not allowing the ball to come into areas around the basket where a shot has a good chance of going in. A forward has to be able to work with the center and the guards in many ways. For example, in switching situations, he has to be quick enough to stay with a guard if he happens to be caught defensing a smaller and faster man. He has to be strong enough to stay with a center—a player who is sometimes an awful lot bigger than he is. The forward's job in defense is very intense and it's a very hard job, because he has to be able to do so many things, and do them from both sides of the court.

Most of you who have picked up this book to learn something about basketball are a long way from being "big men." Yet many of you are big enough—or will be soon—to play the forward or center positions on your team. The one thing that will enable you to play any position well is skill. Basketball demands the development of many skills. It doesn't matter if you can hit ninety-nine percent of your shots from the field, you'll never be on a team if you can't dribble, pass, rebound, and play defense.

So work hard on your game and, whether you play in the backcourt or up front, you'll always make the team.

3. Conditioning

I F   Y O U   W A N T   to be a basketball player you're going to have to be in shape. Playing the game itself will help you accomplish this, but you're going to have to work at staying in shape. Any athlete who is successful at his sport works not only on his skills but also on the ability of his body to perform these skills efficiently.

Basketball is a very demanding game. It puts a large variety of stresses and strains on the body. It requires you to accelerate suddenly and change direction rapidly, to run at top speed for long periods, to leap high after rebounds, and to compete for balls on the floor. Your upper body, arms, and wrists must have the strength and flexibility for passing, shooting, and defensive actions.

Some day you will be one of many boys trying out for a team. You will want everything going for you. Being in shape will help you outperform your teammates, assuming that your skills have been developed equally. You will be faster and stronger, have better reflexes, and better hand-eye coordination.

There are several things a boy can do to get himself in shape for basketball. Running is about the best conditioning exercise we know of. Running develops endurance and builds strong legs, which are necessary for rebounding and getting off on fast breaks. A basketball player often has to run backward. Practice running backward regularly and when you do, make sure to maintain your balance and poise your body as though you were defending against a ball handler.

Another fine exercise for athletes who require endurance and agility is skipping rope. Boxers have known and practiced this for a long time. Practice skipping rope for a few minutes each day and you will find that your leg strength and agility will improve very quickly.

Getting in shape and staying there don't always have to be work. There are many other sports that contribute to quickness, agility, and endurance, and a lot of these are fun to play. Any sport that involves speed, eye-hand coordination, and eye-feet coordination is beneficial. These include handball, tennis, volleyball, and Ping-Pong.

It is a good idea for the serious athlete to ask his school coach or athletic director for a complete physical fitness program if he is not already involved in one.

Earl plays tight defense on the Lakers' Gail Goodrich.

Earl gets a bounce pass past Baltimore's Phil Chenier.

Earl's well-timed, well-executed jump shot is virtually unstoppable.

United Press Internati

A "soft" lay-up, the way Earl does it, is an almost sure two points.

Wes demonstrates the aggressiveness that makes him one of the most dangerous men under the boards in the N.B.A.

Scoring is just one part of the center's offensive responsibility.

Wes muscles the Celtics' Paul Silas.

Wes drives past Dave DeBusschere of the Knicks.

4. Passing

IN BASKETBALL the basic building block of the team game is passing. Every player must be able to pass the ball and catch it properly. Good passing technique starts with a proper grip. Most two-hand passes are done with the ball held in both hands with the fingers spread on either side of the ball and the thumbs in back of the ball. The contact points are the fingers and the thumbs. The palms of the hands make little contact with the ball. This grip provides the best control. Three types of passes that use this grip are the two-handed chest pass, the bounce pass, and the overhead pass. Here's how they are done.

CHEST PASS

The Chest Pass

The chest pass is the simplest yet one of the most useful passes in the game of basketball. Make sure you are holding the ball properly, then bring it up to chest height as you face your teammate. Pass the ball to him by pushing it away from your body as you take a step in the direction of the pass. As you release the ball your arms and fingers should be extended to the fullest as a follow-through action. This enables you to acquire a sensitive feel for the ball as it leaves your fingers—kind of a finger-tip control.

The Bounce Pass

The bounce pass is used in game situations where the chest pass might be intercepted by your opponent. To throw the bounce pass you begin by assuming the same grip that you use for the chest pass. Once again, the ball is brought up to approximately chest height as you face your teammate. Pass the ball to him by bouncing it across the floor and up into his hands. The ball should strike the floor slightly over halfway between you and your teammate. Remember to take a step in the direction of the pass and to extend your arms and fingers fully as you release the ball. The release of the ball is accompanied by a kind of snapping motion of the wrists. This action will cause the ball to develop backspin as it leaves your hands and it will come off the floor at a good angle for your teammate to catch it.

The Overhead Pass

The big man will often use an overhead pass to get the ball down the court after taking a rebound. To throw this pass assume the proper grip, then raise the ball over your head in both hands. As you throw the ball to your teammate lean forward and take a step in the direction of the pass.

Other passes that you will learn to use include the overhand baseball-type pass, in which the ball is shifted to one hand and thrown like a baseball to your teammate, and the shovel pass, in which the ball is shoveled in an underhand fashion to your teammate.

You should keep some things in mind when it is necessary to pass the ball in a game. For example, you should try to use short passes because they are less likely to be intercepted. Your opponent is go-

OVERHEAD PASS

ing to be watching your eyes, so try to confuse him by looking in one direction and passing in another. Make sure the spot to which you pass the ball is one from which your teammate can get a shot off. You are not helping him if you pass to his blind spot or to his back.

Don't underrate the importance of passing. Passing is the fastest way to advance the ball down the court. It is going to take a great deal of practice to make you an effective passer. You are going to have to get out on the court with your teammates and practice the various types of passes. Basketball is a game of constant motion, so you and your teammates should move around constantly, passing the ball from one to the other. When passing, remember to lead your receiver if he is moving down the court and to keep the ball out in front of him so he can control it immediately and get the shot off.

When you practice passing, it is desirable to simulate game conditions as much as possible. Some of the drills in Chapter Twelve will show the kind of movement, dribbling, and passing you will experience in a game.

5. Dribbling

I F Y O U H A V E ever seen a great dribbler on the court, someone who is a real artist, you have probably been motivated to learn this exciting part of the game. Dribbling is fun to do and exciting to watch but one of the dangers is that boys sometimes tend to overdo it. Dribbling, like all the other basketball skills you will be learning, is a vital part of the game and should be used at the appropriate time in the game, not as a way for a player to show off.

In order to learn to dribble properly, approach this skill slowly and precisely. Dribbling is done with the fingers, not with the palms of the hands.

DRIBBLING

Do not slap at the ball, but control it delicately with your fingers and the flexing action of your wrist. When you dribble the ball down the court, you should be in good dribbling posture. This means that your back should be straight, you should be bent forward slightly at the knees, you should be up on the balls of your feet, and, very important, your head should be up and your eyes moving around the court.

Once you get the feel of controlling the ball with your fingertips, start moving around the court with it. Move slowly at first, then gradually increase your speed. Practice moving in a counterclockwise direction, then switch off and move in a clockwise direction. The more skillful you become at dribbling the more versatile a player you will be. To be truly mobile on the court, you have to be able to dribble equally well with both hands. You can develop your own drills that will include switching hands, changing direction, and changing your rate of speed as you move down the court.

One final thing to remember is to be alert to what is happening around you on the court as you move with the ball. As soon as you come to a stop, look for an open man and pass the ball to him immediately.

Here's a summary of points to keep in mind

when you are dribbling in a game or a practice session:

Control the ball with your fingertips and wrist action, not with the palms of the hands.

Keep your back straight and your head up, eyes moving around the court.

Learn to dribble equally well with both hands.

Learn to change direction and speed as you dribble.

Protect the ball with your body when you dribble.

6. Shooting

As the word basketball implies, the object of the game is to put the ball in the basket. Since you win a basketball game by outscoring your opponent, shooting is the most important thing that you do on the basketball court. Shooting is also the most personal part of the game. The way a player shoots the basketball is determined by his physical size and strength, his natural feel for the shot, and perhaps, to some extent, by his personality.

Many players have developed odd styles of shooting. Dick Barnett, for example, shoots his jump shot in what appears to be an off-balance position. He seems to be falling over, yet the ball goes into the basket. Jerry West, on the other hand, is a picture-type ballplayer and shoots with a classic style. Since most of you are starting from scratch as new players, you should try to learn the tested techniques that have been developed by the great shooters in the game.

Before approaching specific shots, let's consider some general ideas on shooting. Concentration, for example, is vital for good shooting. There will be many factors on the court that will tend to distract you from your shooting. The pressures of the game, the harassment of defensive players, the noise of the crowds are all things you must deal with. So concentrate. Although your shooting technique will become mechanical, each shot is a deliberate action.

At first, learn the shots required by the position you play and the shots most suited to your physical make-up. But never stop learning new shots. By perfecting the shots you know and by attempting always to learn new ones, you will build a repertory of shots which will make you very hard to defense.

A good place to begin to learn to shoot is at the free throw line.

The Free Throw

You have probably noticed that basketball play-

FREE THROW—WES'S STYLE

ers use a wide variety of free-throw styles. Many players and coaches feel that the foul line is the place where you can do your own thing as long as you can get the ball in the basket with consistency. There is much to be said, however, for building your free-throw technique around the form you will use for your jump shot. The closer you keep these two shots in style the more you will be able to control them and score with them consistently.

Do you remember the first pointer you received on dribbling? You were told to control the ball with your fingers, not with the palms of your hands. Grip the ball so it is supported by the pads of the fingers of your shooting hand. The other hand is the support hand and should be placed slightly to the front of the ball. Your elbows should be kept comfortably close to your body. Check to be sure an imaginary line running from the elbow of your shooting hand through the V formed by the thumb and index finger of your shooting hand would run in a straight line to the basket.

If you are a right-handed shooter, your right foot should be advanced slightly and pointed directly at the basket. If you point your left foot to the left at about a forty-five degree angle you will find that you will be comfortable and will be able to maintain your balance throughout the shot. Your knees

FREE THROW—EARL'S STYLE

should be slightly flexed and your body relaxed. At the moment before the shot, the ball should be at eye height, the wrist of the shooting hand cocked back, and your eyes concentrating on a point just beyond the rim. When you shoot the ball, don't think of throwing it but rather of launching it toward the basket, using legs, body, arm, wrist, and fingers. The ball should roll off your fingertips as it leaves your hand. This will apply backspin to the ball, which will help it drop into the basket should it hit the rim. Follow through as though you were reaching out for the rim of the basket with the fingertips of your shooting hand.

The Jump Shot

The jump shot allows you, the shooter, to get the ball up and over the defensive man attempting to block the shot. It is the most widely used shot in basketball since even the smaller player becomes a scoring threat if he is proficient at it. The stance for the jump shot is slightly different from that for the free throw. When you set up for a jump shot, your feet should be spread apart about the same distance as the width of your shoulders. Your entire body should be square to the target and the

JUMP SHOT

toes of both feet should be pointed approximately at the basket. To get the shot off, flex your knees, bring the ball into aiming position as you did with the free throw, cock the wrist of your shooting hand, then leap up. As you reach the high point of your jump, propel the ball toward the basket using the arm-wrist-finger action previously described. A good checkpoint for this shot is to make sure that the elbow of your shooting hand points at the basket and leads the shot prior to the uncocking of the wrist.

The Hook Shot

If you have ever seen Kareem Jabbar or Wilt Chamberlain mount a hook-shot attack, you know that this shot can be virtually impossible to defense. Of course, even this shot has its limitations. It is most effective when used by a center or a big forward in an area fairly close to the basket.

To shoot the hook shot, stand with your back to the basket. If someone is guarding you, remember to protect the ball by keeping your body between the defender and the ball. If you are a right-handed shooter, begin the shot by taking a step away from the basket with your left foot. Bring your shooting

HOOK SHOT

arm up over your head as you rotate your head toward the basket and focus on your target, a spot either on the backboard or just beyond the rim of the basket. Keep your shooting arm fully extended throughout this shot and follow through toward the basket after releasing the ball.

The hook shot is a very difficult shot and will require a great deal of practice if you are going to use it effectively in a game.

The Set Shot

At one time the two-handed set shot, also known as the chest shot, was the most widely used shot in the game. Not too many players use this shot today. The jump shot gives the shooter a better chance of getting the ball over the defender's outstretched arms. But who knows? Perhaps the set shot will enjoy a comeback. It's a good shot for accuracy.

To throw a two-handed set shot, hold the ball at chest height with your elbows in close to your body. Flex your knees before the shot since much of the power will be generated by your legs. As your knees unflex, launch the ball toward the basket by extending your arms toward the target. Re-

LAY-UP FROM FRONT OF BASKET

member what you learned about releasing the ball from your fingertips with wrist action.

Variations of the two-handed set shot include the one-handed set shot and the overhead set shot.

The Lay-up

If your team is successful in getting a man down the court on a fast break, he will be in a position to use the surest shot in basketball—the lay-up. The lay-up is just what the words say. It is laying the ball up into the basket. As a young player, you should plan to bank all your lay-ups off the backboard. Later on, when you are taller and have more control, you may want to make lay-ups by dropping the ball cleanly over the rim. Making this shot is really quite simple. Dribble down the court until you approach the basket, then plant your foot and go up as high as possible, laying the ball against the backboard as gently as possible. As you approach the basket and go up for the shot, keep your eyes on the spot on the backboard against which you wish to lay the ball. The softer you make this shot the more chance it has of being successful.

Tips to Remember

Here are some general tips on shooting that summarize what you should know to be a good shooter:

Learn to make all your shots and your lay-ups with either hand.

Concentrate on releasing the ball with a delicate wrist-finger action so that accuracy results and backspin is generated.

Learn to get your shots off quickly so that your opponent cannot defense you effectively.

Make sure to maintain proper stance, footwork, and balance during your shots.

Always, always follow through.

LAY-UP FROM THE SIDE

7. Individual's Offense

OFFENSE IN BASKETBALL is putting to-
gether the individual skills to score points for the
team. There is really no such thing as *individual*
offense; this is a contradiction of ideas. But there
are things a player must do as an individual if he
is going to be a valuable team player.

You are going to be continually confronted
with one-on-one situations during a game. This is
your personal contest and one that you must win.

A good base on which to build an offense is
speed. Each individual on a team must agree that
this is the kind of game your team will play and
each player must be sufficiently conditioned. A
fast, moving offense will be a strong challenge to
your opponent. The New York Knicks have built

an offensive philosophy on speed, movement, and teamwork. This combination can be the first step in developing your offensive style. Play brightly, alertly, and fast. Pass quickly when you stop dribbling if you don't have a shot. Get down the court quickly when your team gets the ball. Keep moving whether you have the ball or not and keep your opponent moving; let him know that it won't be easy to stay with you.

There are some techniques you have to develop to come out on top in one-on-one situations. Let's examine some of them.

Pivoting

The pivot allows you to move your body around a spot on the court as long as one foot remains in contact with the floor. This foot is called the pivot foot.

If you receive a pass while both feet are on the floor, then either foot can be the pivot foot. When you move one foot, the other foot is established as the pivot foot. If you are moving down the court while dribbling, the first foot to contact the floor when you come to a stop is the pivot foot. The pivot is used to protect the ball. It is especially

THE DRIVING SHOT

effective when you want to pass the ball to a teammate. The moment you come to a stop, swing your
body around on the ball of your pivot foot so your
body is between your opponent and the ball. Bend
forward at the waist and keep your elbows out.
This keeps the defensive man away from the ball
and allows you to pass off to a teammate.

Driving

In order to drive past your opponent to score,
you are going to have to manipulate him into making a mistake. Most of the good one-on-one players
are adept at forcing their opponents to make mis-
takes. For instance, if you receive a pass, don't
dribble the ball unless you are going to advance it
immediately. As your guard approaches you, fake
a jump shot. If he commits to blocking the shot,
you've got him. Since you haven't used up your
dribble, you can drive past him for the lay-up. If he
doesn't react to the fake you can take the shot next
time.

If your opponent is guarding you closely and
you don't have a shot, you've got to make him react
to one side so you can drive around him to the
other side. Hold the ball at chest height with both

hands. As your man approaches, look to the right, step out with your right foot, and move the ball and your body as though you were going to charge in that direction. As the defensive man reacts to your move, swing the ball and your body to the left, pivoting on your left foot (your pivot foot). Your first step is with your right foot. Get as far around your opponent as possible with this first step. Don't give him a chance to recover. Here's where your dribbling practice will reward you. You will have to dribble with your left hand to keep your body between your opponent and the ball. Now drive to the basket for two points.

Screens

A tactic often used to frustrate a man-to-man defense is the screen. In this technique an offensive player is positioned to prevent a defensive opponent from covering his man, who is either driving for the basket or in the act of shooting. If the driving player can gain a step or so on his opponent, he can cut around his teammate, who becomes a roadblock in the path of the defensive man.

In Chapter 10, Team Offense, the screen is described as it is used in specific plays.

8. Defense

Every team has had the experience of not being able to score effectively in a game. Nothing goes in. As they say, "There's a lid on the basket." This is when defense has to win it for you.

Defense is a less chancy element of the game than shooting. Defense depends on a constant, aggressive, alert challenge to the opposing team. Defense doesn't even require a particularly talented player. Usually, the high scorer on a team is a "natural shooter," a boy who has developed his instinct for shooting. The defensive star on a team —the guy who can stop the opponent's high scorer —may be an average athlete who has developed his defensive ability through determination and hard work.

Defense, from the team standpoint, means pressure. Pressure is the key word, the key thought. Each boy on a defensive team must be mentally conditioned and physically able to apply pressure to the opponent throughout the game. Harass the shooter on every shot, try to block or intercept every pass, challenge the dribbler and try to take the ball away from him, and, finally, take away the second shot. If the shot is missed, make sure your team gets the rebound. Take away the opponent's offense in any way you can.

Stance

The most effective stance for the defensive man is the one that presents the greatest obstacle to the offensive man. If your opponent is not in shooting position, situate yourself in front of him between him and the basket. You should be balanced on the balls of your feet—never get caught flatfooted. Lean forward at the waist with your arms outstretched to obstruct passes.

Move with your man while concentrating on staying between him and the basket. If he moves to either side, try to stay with him by sliding or shuffling your feet sideways. Don't cross one leg over

the other. Your opponent may fake you into this position then take off the other way.

When your opponent is within shooting range, your stance changes somewhat. Face your opponent with one foot advanced. If your right foot is the forward foot raise your right hand to obstruct your opponent's view of the basket and, of course, to block any attempted shot. Your left arm should be extended out to the side to guard against passes. Remember to keep your balance so you will be mobile and able to play your man tightly.

Be an aggressive defensive player. Take the ini-

GOOD DEFENSE—A BLOCKED SHOT

tiative away from the offense as much as possible. You do this in several ways. Make certain that you always have your hand in your opponent's face. Always try to have a hand in the passing lane. Look for opportunities to get the ball away from him.

You and your teammates should attempt to prevent the offense from sticking to their offensive pattern. For example, if they like to work their plays out of the pivot, concentrate on keeping the ball away from their pivot man. If they are hurting you from the outside, don't let their outside shooter get set on the floor. Play him aggressively and harass his shooting.

A defensive device that you can work on is defending against the dribbler. Practice this with a teammate until you can stop him from advancing the ball past you while dribbling. This takes away a valuable part of your opponents' offense in a game situation.

A pressure-type defense means playing your man aggressively even when he doesn't have the ball. You must stay with your man at all times. Position yourself between him and the ball. This means always knowing where the ball is. Attempt to intercept or deflect any pass to your man. In short, try to keep him out of the play.

9. Rebounding

R EBOUNDING OFF the defensive boards is primarily a job for the big man. He has to get the ball for his team and get it out quickly. Smaller men also have to be alert during rebound situations. Their speed and reactions will often get them to the ball first. In any case, every player can and should try to position himself to prevent his man from getting to the ball.

Here are some tips for rebounding. They'll be especially useful for the big man, but they are fundamentals that any player can benefit from.

Get There First

It is possible to develop an instinct for anticipating where the ball is going to be after a shot. The first thing you do is treat every shot as though it were going to be missed. The ball's going to come off the rim and you've got to get to it. But where is it going to come down?

It takes an average of three seconds for the ball to leave the shooter's hand, form its arc to the basket, hit the rim, bounce to its highest point, and start its descent to the point where you can reach it. Now you know when it's going to arrive, but you still don't know where.

Learning this is a matter of studying shots from various angles. For example, if a shot is made from the right-hand side of the goal, about seventy percent of the time it will rebound long and come off the left side. Naturally, the reverse is true. A good rebounder makes a mental note of every shot and how it comes off the rim. Before long, you develop the ability to make an automatic mental calculation that can point you to the right spot.

Count to yourself as the shot leaves the shooter's hands: *1001 . . . 1002 . . . 1003*. You know where the ball should be coming down and you'll be there at the right time. The chances are, however, that you'll find yourself in a traffic jam. That part of the court is going to be pretty well clogged up.

REBOUNDING

Establish Your Position

When you move into the area where the ball should be coming down, you have to establish yourself there. A lot of bodies will be pushing around, so you've got to be prepared to hold your position. It's like defending territory. Once you get it, it's yours and you don't want anyone else coming in. You have to make yourself as strong and as wide as you can. Use your bulk; keep your elbows out. Prepare to spring with both legs under you, then go up aggressively to meet the ball.

When you get the ball, protect it by pivoting, if necessary, to place your body between the ball and your opponent; then get it out as quickly as you can to initiate the fast break.

If you see that you are not going to get the rebound, concentrate on blocking your man so that he doesn't get it. Do this by positioning yourself in his path to the ball. Keep your body between your opponent and the basket.

Offensive Rebounding

When one of your teammates is shooting, you have an advantage over your opponent. You play along with your teammates all the time. You know what kind of shots they like to take, and you know what shots they can make as well as the ones they're apt to miss. If you make a real effort to study your teammates' shooting styles, it will truly help you in offensive rebounding.

Once the shot is in the air, all the principles of defensive rebounding apply—with one exception. You may have an opportunity for a tip-in on a missed shot.

Tip-in

The center and big forwards are going to be right in the heart of the action under the offensive boards. They should be adept at tipping so that no opportunity to score is wasted.

The tip-in is done with the arm extended over-head and is accomplished mostly with the wrist and fingers. The player must time his jump per-fectly so that he meets the ball as it comes off the rim or backboard and guides it into the basket.

10. Team Offense

N O W   T H A T   you have developed some proficiency at passing, dribbling, and shooting, you will want to put these new skills to work.

Even if you and your friends are not playing organized basketball, you should start to learn some of the basic offenses. When you and your teammates get together, start practicing some of these offenses. You'll discover that they will add more fun and excitement to the game.

Let's start out with the fast break; this one is not too difficult to learn.

The Fast Break

The fast break (Diagram A) begins as soon as the defensive team gets possession of the ball,

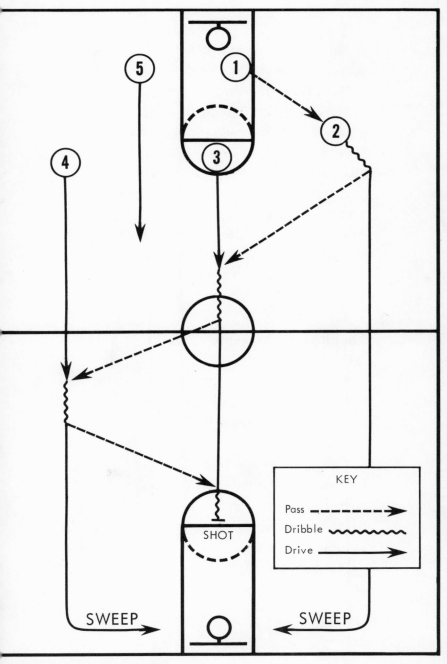

KEY

Pass -------→

Dribble ～～～→

Drive ———→

SHOT

SWEEP →

← SWEEP

DIAGRAM A   **FAST BREAK**

either by interception, defensive rebound, or following an opponent's score.

The play starts when Player 1 takes the rebound and gives Player 2 a quick outlet pass. Player 2 passes to 3, 3 to 4, who throws it back to 3. Player 3 stops at the foul line if he cannot drive all the way to the basket. He then shoots or passes to one of the sweep men, 2 or 4, who must square the corners. Player 5 trails the play. If the fast break scoring attempt fails, a set offensive pattern is started with Player 1 coming downcourt after defending against the interception.

The Single-Post Offense

It's not always going to be possible to set up a fast break and, even when you do, it won't always be successful. Most of the time a set offense must be employed.

The single-post offense is a good one to learn because it provides each position with an equal opportunity to score. This prevents the defense from concentrating on one or two outstanding scorers. Each man should be allowed to pass, drive, or shoot anytime he finds the opportunity to do any of those things successfully. We will explore this

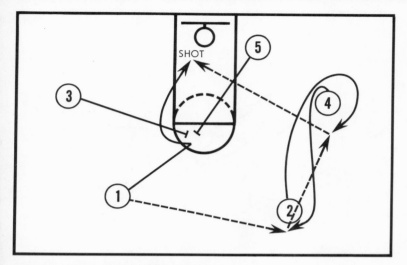

DIAGRAM B **GUARD'S PLAY**

offense from the standpoint of each position beginning with the guard.

GUARD'S PLAY

The play (Diagram B) begins with Guard 1 passing to Forward 4 who has changed positions with Guard 2 on the weak side. Player 2 is now at the forward position. The Center 5 breaks to the high post (the area in the key beyond the foul line); Forward 3 also breaks to the high post to form a double screen with Center 5. Forward 4 passes the ball to Guard 2 who is at forward position. Guard 1 hesitates a moment, waiting for the double screen to form; then he breaks off the double screen running his defensive man into the

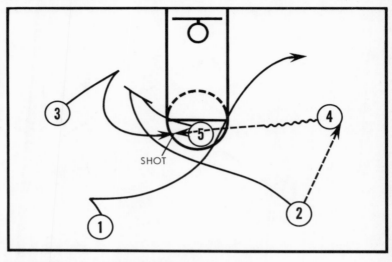

DIAGRAM C **FORWARD'S PLAY**

screen. He receives the pass from Guard 2 for an easy shot underneath.

FORWARD'S PLAY

This play (Diagram C) begins with Guard 2 passing the ball to Forward 4. He then crosses the top of the key to set up a double screen at the high post with Center 5 on Player 3's man. Center 5 waits for Guard 2 to come to him and they set up a screen together. Guard 1 cuts to the strong side (the side where most of the offensive men are concentrated) at the baseline, timing his cut by Guard 2 as Guard 2 is running to the weak side. Forward 3 has faked his defensive man down low on the baseline running him into the double screen set by

98

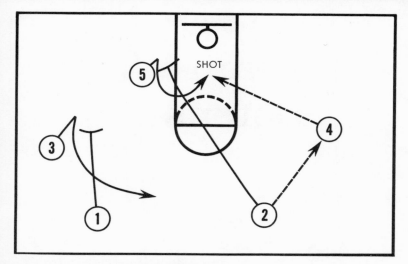

DIAGRAM D **CENTER'S PLAY**

Guard 2 and Center 5. Forward 4, who has received the pass, hesitates for the screen to develop. He takes one dribble to the middle of the court and passes to Forward 3 who is coming off the screen to shoot at the foul line.

CENTER'S PLAY—LOW POST

The play (Diagram D) begins with Guard 2 passing the ball to Forward 4 and then screening away Center 5's defensive man. Center 5 comes off Guard 2's screen, receives the pass from Forward 4 at the low post for the easy shot. (The low post is the area in the key inside the foul line.) Guard 1 and Forward 3 exchange positions on the weak side to keep their defensive men occupied.

11. Team Defense

THE DEFENSIVE SKILLS you are learning are useful in a one-on-one situation. In a game, you and your teammates will be challenging another organized group of players. These players will have devised and practiced offensive tactics that they believe will enable them to outscore your team. Now your individual defensive skills must become part of a group effort. Since you are countering an organized attack, your defense must be organized to be effective.

If you watch professional basketball, you may have noticed that we play a man-to-man-type defense. Your coach at school will probably use some variations of the zone defense. Here's how both types of defense work.

Zone Defense

The purpose of defense is to prevent the offensive team from scoring. The zone defenses attempt to do this by establishing all five defensive men as a movable unit that always directs its strength to the ball. Each player in a zone defense is responsible for a certain area and the men in that area, instead of being responsible for an individual player. Each zone man guards players who come into his zone and strives to prevent shots and passes in this defensive area. A zone defense, to be effective, must set up as a unit and wait for the offense.

Most zone defenses are what we call shifting defenses. This means that they key on the ball first and then the men as they move into the defensive areas. All types of zones are compact formations of players working together as total defensive systems. The entire team shifts quickly as a unit to the side of the court where the ball is in play. The defensive men must stay in a compact formation defending all openings or lanes through which a smart offensive team might be able to work the ball.

There are several types of zones and many variations. However, in all zones the position of the lines of defense will depend on the offensive strat-

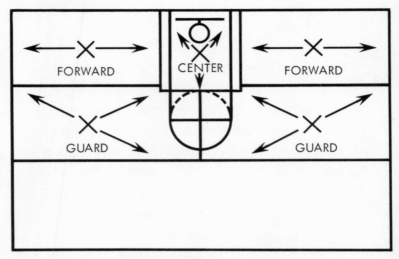

DIAGRAM E **2-1-2 ZONE DEFENSE**

egy employed. Remember, zone defenses always attempt to shift strong to the ball.

Here are some samples of zone defenses that you'll see used by school teams.

2-1-2 ZONE DEFENSE

This is perhaps the most widely used zone defense. The 2-1-2 (Diagram E) provides good coverage of all the potential scoring zones rather than concentrating on one area or scoring zone. It provides sound coverage of the very important foul line area and also insures good rebounding protection. You'll note that the 2-1-2 zone puts the defensive team in excellent position to start a fast-

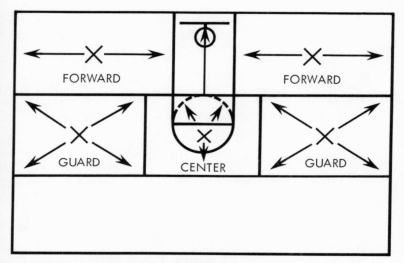

DIAGRAM F   **3-2 ZONE DEFENSE**

break offensive attack. The 2-1-2 is very effective against teams that rely on working inside as their basic offensive attack.

3-2 ZONE DEFENSE

The 3-2 zone (Diagram F) is the most effective zone defense against a good outside shooting team. This zone will also force the offensive team into more ball handling, which will eventually result in turnovers. If there is no threat of a corner shooting attack, this defense will be strong for rebounding and getting the ball out quickly for the fast break.

Man-to-Man Defense

The man-to-man defense makes it possible to match players against opponents of equal size, skill, and speed. Each player is assigned to a certain opponent and he is responsible for him defensively. The player who holds his opponent scoreless or to a few points, while outscoring him, is a valuable team man.

Man-to-man defense requires each player to be able to guard his man in all defensive situations and to be skilled in defensive fundamentals: establishing good position, proper stance, good body balance, defensive fakes, good peripheral vision, good hand and arm movement, and ability to move with his opponent, blocking the shooting and passing lanes without fouling.

One weakness of the man-to-man defense is that screens can be set to free the offensive man from his defender. Good offensive moves will make it very difficult at times for a defender to stay between his man and the most direct line to the basket. The defensive team must have a definite plan to meet the various offensive picks and screens. Verbal calls to alert a teammate to screens and picks are essential in the man-to-man defense.

There are several variations to the basic man-to-man defense. One of these is the *switching man-to-man,* which means that the defensive men switch assignments when a teammate is in trouble or loses his man. Another variation is the *tight man-to-man,* which requires that a defender never leave or switch his man on defense. A third variation is the *loose man-to-man.* This defense is used against a weak outside shooting team and is a kind of combination of zone and man-to-man play.

The man-to-man defenses and their variations generally require players with advanced skills. Another technique requiring experienced players is the press.

The Press

You may have heard the expression *full court press* in connection with defensive basketball. John Wooden, coach of the UCLA team, was the pioneer of the full court zone press.

When employing the press, the UCLA team sets up its zone after scoring as the opposing team prepares to inbound the ball. Two men set up on either side of the foul circle at the end of the court where the ball is being inbounded. Their job is to put instant pressure on the man receiving the inbound pass. Two more men are situated on either side of the court halfway between the foul circle and the center line. Their responsibility is to pick up a man driving down the court with the ball and to defend against passes into this middle area. The fifth man, normally the center, sets up in the vicinity of the center line. He picks up any man with the ball who has managed to penetrate into his area. He also looks to intercept passes coming down court.

The purpose of the press is to begin to harass the offensive team the moment they inbound the ball. This type of defense aims to disrupt the opponents' game by preventing them from setting up their offensive patterns.

12. Practice

PRACTICE SHOULD BE undertaken on two levels: individual practice and organized team practice.

If you have a basketball court available to practice on, or even a hoop in your backyard, you can continually work on your shooting. There is always room for improvement in shooting. You will want to sharpen up your free throws and your jump shot.

Practice your jump shot from various spots on the court. If you are not hitting consistently, find out why. You may have developed some of these common shooting errors: faulty grip, faulty stance, failure to aim properly, faulty balance, incorrect release, faulty arc to basket, failure to follow through.

Perfect form on a Monroe jump shot.

During your individual practice sessions, you can work on your dribbling and driving. This means practicing fakes, changes of speed and direction, and dribbling with both hands.

Drills

We have selected some drills for you and your teammates or friends to use when you get together for a practice session. These drills are truly valuable for any group of players who want to be able to work together as a unit.

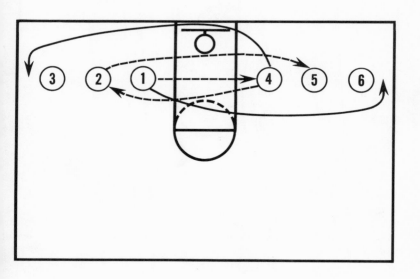

PASSING—CROSSOVER

Player 1 passes to 4; 4 passes to 2; 2 passes to 5 and so on. Players go to their right to the end of the opposite line after passing the ball. The two-hand chest pass should be used, followed by the two-hand bounce pass, and then the baseball pass.

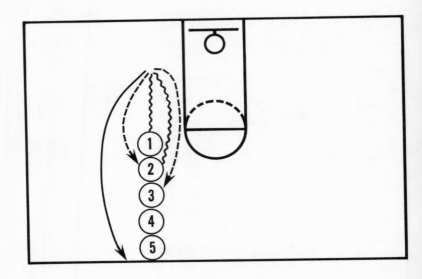

DRIBBLE—PASS

Player 1 dribbles out ten to fifteen feet, pivots around and passes to 2; 2 dribbles out, pivots, and passes to 3. As he completes the pass, each player goes to the end of the line. This procedure is repeated until each player has participated. Use all three types of passes.

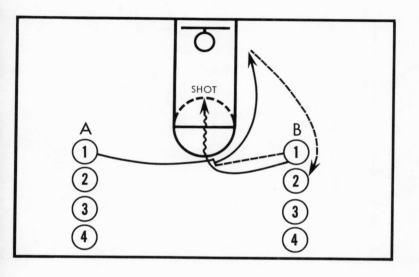

GIVE-AND-GO SHOOTING

Player 1 in line B passes to player 1 in line A as A1 cuts across in position at the head of the key. A1 gives B1 a hand-off pass. B1 dribbles to the basket for a lay-up or jump-shot. A1 goes to the boards for the ball and passes it back out to B2. The procedure is repeated and players switch lines to give everyone a chance to shoot and rebound.

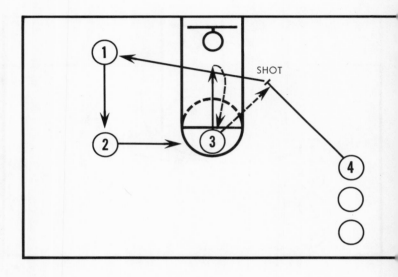

SPEED PASS AND SHOOT

Player 3 passes to 4 coming in for a shot. As the pass is made, 1 moves to 2's position. Player 2 moves to 3's position. Player 4 takes the shot and moves to 1's position. Player 3 rebounds and passes to 2, then 3 goes to the end of the line. Player 2 passes to 1, 1 passes to 3, 3 passes to 4. Players rotate positions.

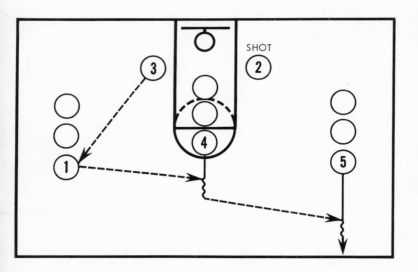

FAST BREAK

Player 2 shoots ball against backboard. Player 3 rebounds and passes the ball out to 1 who immediately passes to 4. Player 4 breaks straight up the floor looking to pass to 1 or 5 who are breaking down the outsides.

We believe basketball has something to offer every boy. For some of you it will be an enjoyable way to pass the time after school and stay in shape. Other boys will make the school team and work toward and perhaps earn a college scholarship. Maybe some of you will be the pros of tomorrow.

No matter what role basketball plays in your life, you will want to excel as a player. So work on your game. Practice your shooting. Participate in the drills. But most of all, play plenty of basketball.

EARL MONROE

Described by many as the most exciting player in the game, Earl Monroe is usually among the league's top scorers. As a college senior at Winston-Salem, Earl averaged 41.5 points per game, shot an incredible .606% from the field and became the nation's all-time single-season scoring champion with 1,329 points. He was the Bullets' first draft choice in 1967 and went on to win Rookie of the Year honors. After four seasons with Baltimore, Monroe joined the New York Knickerbockers in 1971.

WES UNSELD

Wes Unseld, after an illustrious college career at Louisville, joined the Baltimore Bullets in 1968. He became only the second player in history to be named Rookie of the Year and Most Valuable Player. As a first-year man, Wes was also named to the All-Pro and All-Rookie teams and selected as basketball's top performer by the Academy of Professional Sports. Wes, with his ability to get the ball off the boards and set up the fast break, is recognized as the key to the continual success of the Baltimore Bullets.

RAY SIEGENER

Ray Siegener has edited and written several books on sports.